Nocturnal
Sunrise

Nocturnal Sunrise

ALISON STRANGE-GREEN

To order additional copies of this book, contact:
Xlibris Corporation
0-800-644-6988
www.xlibrispublishing.co.uk
Orders@xlibrispublishing.co.uk
302822

Dedicated to:

Michael for giving me the inspiration and Alexander and Isabella for being so patient.

Contents

Summers Day 11

Time 12

Broken 13

Adrift 14

Bleakness 15

The Breeze 16

Captured 17

Close to me 18

Clouds 19

Delights 20

Imagine 21

Immorality 22

Landscape 23

Moonlight 24

Ravaged 25

Reputations 26

Shimmering 27

Smile 28

Sword 29

The Abyss 30

The Cascade 31

The Howling 33

Frosted 34

Harmony 35

The Bedroom 36

Crashed 37

Days 38

Empty 39

Frozen 40

Reflections 41

Tortured 42

Twisted 43

Delusions 49

Deity 50
Cherubs 51
Euphoria... 52
Church 53
Hope 54
Leaves 55
Salvation... 56
Soulless... 57
The Mist 58
Crucifixion 64
Depictions... 65
Grin 67
Inferno.. 68
Peaceful Revenge 69
Shallow grave.. 70
Spectre 71
The Statue... 72
Ponder.. 73
Suffering... 74
Worthless 75
The Graveyard.. 81
The Count 82
Chamber... 83
Not shiny or happy!.. 85
Kings and Queens... 86
Discord... 88
Yesterday 94
Aching.. 95
Choices... 96
Crossroads 97
Devolution 98
Distrust... 99
Incantations.. 100
Normality 101
Passing 102
Sloth... 103

Sullied 104
Truth 105
Wilderness 106
Wounded 107
Babble 113
Blinding Light.. 115
Cobbled Road.. 116
Dreams 117
Honesty 118
Regression 119
Solace... 120
Sparkle 121
Destructive.. 122
Shadows 123
Tears.. 124
Unfinished eternity.. 125
Summerland... 127
Heinous 128
Effigy... 129
Oblivion.. 130
Misery 131
Heretics 132

Summers Day

Love shone between the murky clouds
One fine summer's day
I gave you all the love I had
Only to take it all away

Angels danced inside my heart
Now only to rear their heads

Love it shines so dimly
In every single way
Replaced slowly by the tears
Thoughts of one fine summer's day

Nocturnal Sunrise
ALISON STRANGE-GREEN

11

Time

Forever facing backwards
The forward facing crowds
Across the darkened laden muse
Empty shadows cast

Blistering shadows of the rain
A mist that turns to dust
Forever virtuous, silent
images in stones of love

Nocturnal Sunrise
ALISON STRANGE-GREEN

Broken

*"Within the deepest minds
The darkest souls hurt
Each blackened sun is divine"*

Nocturnal Sunrise
ALISON STRANGE-GREEN

Adrift

Bleeding souls are broken
Sirens lost at sea
Dizzy heights of yesterday
Only vibrant dreams

Dirty, vivid, dusty voids
Crippled, ravaged bones
Soulless depths of ignorance
Glimmering, shivering cold

Grotesque happiness laid bare
Meaningless pots of gold
Thousand waves crashed ashore
A view I cannot behold

I only cast a glance once more
My memory, empty
Thoughts of ragged images
Of yesterday's unwanted dream

Nocturnal Sunrise
ALISON STRANGE-GREEN

Bleakness

Bleakness of the winter
Sparkle of the rays
Turned your heart to ice
Sunny days to a violent haze

Between the snowflakes flittered
Fragmented thoughts of me
Destiny retained itself
Crashing through the trees

Each flake settles on your face
To abandon you in turn
Compared the love that left our lives
Never to return

The darkest day and hour
Each crystal, lucid lake
Every honeysuckle sky that followed
Regrets of that fateful day

Nocturnal Sunrise
ALISON STRANGE-GREEN

15

The Breeze

Directions change like the wind
Flowers wither and fade
Where fairies gathered golden flakes
Only bedraggled weeds cascade

Morning light caught a blossom
to shed a single tear
Ravaged by its memories
A garden steeped in fear

Of blissful time in happiness
Lovingly destroyed with cheer
Memories blown in the breeze
Recollections of holding you near

Nocturnal Sunrise
ALISON STRANGE-GREEN

Captured

Days of walking through the rain
Slowly turned to night
Every moment captured
willingness inside

Moonlit nights on empty shores
Revealed sickened tales
Sadness on the beaches
Foreboding of the waves

Tragic lovers lost at sea
The ocean took its prey
Ghastly scenes of yesterday
By night, just not by day

The sun it rose without fear
Illuminated the skies
Reflection on bluest oceans
came harrowing, chilling cries

Nocturnal Sunrise
ALISON STRANGE-GREEN

Close to me

Waiting quietly by your side
A mesmerising stare
Thoughts rush aimlessly
through my mind
Of days when you were there

Tomorrows just another day
without you close to me
Tranquil seas hold my thoughts
for all eternity

Shallow waters running deep
Every tearful gaze
Remembering days of careless ways
when you were close to me

Nocturnal Sunrise
ALISON STRANGE-GREEN

Clouds

Alone we are falling
Together as one
Heartfelt reflections
Seasons of love

Birds within a storm
Lost and hidden from view
Twisted old images
Bitter memories of you

Many words spoken
without a sound
Tumbling from grace
Deepest of rain clouds

A feeling never lost
Most dazzling of rays
Through tearful eyes
Yet bright sunny days

Nocturnal Sunrise
ALISON STRANGE-GREEN

Delights

Cradled by the sounds of life
All beauty shed a tear
Blizzards beckon faithlessly
Clouds gathered far and near

Soulless hearts within statues
started to beat at dawn
Carved in stone an effigy
embraced the raging storm

Sentimental holiness
blowing with delights
Messages of yesteryears
regained a heavenly sunrise

Nocturnal Sunrise
ALISON STRANGE-GREEN

Imagine

Imagine all tomorrows
fade solemnly unto the sky
Passing rays of summer sun
were cast upon each smile

Words whispered graciously
Full of doubtful quivering fear
The sun it laughed no longer
Replaced by humiliation and tears

Compensated by swirling winds
Nature changed it course
With it bringing loneliness
Shallowness and discord

Similar are the seasons
Not unlike a waning heart
Admiration turns to neutrality
Converting sunshine into the dark

Nocturnal Sunrise
ALISON STRANGE-GREEN

Immorality

Crimson shades of violent red
immersed into the sea
Slowly sweeping, darkening
A revulsion plain to see

Turning crystal, deep blue oceans
into a blood red grave
The moon lit each scarlet wave
turning calm waters into rage

A Flickering, sanguine sea
reaching slowly to the shore
Existence of the sacred ones
was to remain no more

Illuminate the waters
Was the deathly slaughter seen?
Humanity butchered innocence
Revealing immorality

Nocturnal Sunrise
ALISON STRANGE-GREEN

Landscape

Pencil drawings
etched in gold
Stories ancient
gratuitous and bold

Past lives in pleasure
Insufferable pain
Desolate landscapes
Warm summer's rain

All is left
of this great effigy
Written in gold
what we're meant to believe

Memories tarnished
desecrated with time
Eternal cities consumed
Truths in your mind

Nocturnal Sunrise
ALISON STRANGE-GREEN

Moonlight

Embers and ashes
So do they rise
Sunrise foreboding
Where is the moonlight?

Colours alluring
lustrous and bright
Scintillating yellows
seeping through the night

Golden and glimmering
Past this I see
A void full of shadows
desolate and empty

Frozen and astray
Darkness of the gloom
Yearning for sobriety
in dark sober tones

Taking solace and pleasure
nestled in the unknown
Crushed into oblivion
Darkness turns golden

An entity at best
falls through the night
Where is the comfort, my security?
Where is my moonlight?

Nocturnal Sunrise
ALISON STRANGE-GREEN

Ravaged

Smiling eyes and weeping brows
Jewels in the sea
Slightly jaded looks of gold
You were my destiny

The cresting moon faded
Rainbows preceded the rain
Gladly passing glances
Hearts tormented, sharing pain

Magnificence and wonder
were just a parody
Stars twinkled brightly
You were my destiny

Places lost in time once more
Understanding thoughts
Together torn and ravaged
Bringing sadness and remorse

Ships in the darkness
drifting no particular course
Sadness stole the stars
Isolation reigns once more

Nocturnal Sunrise
ALISON STRANGE-GREEN

Reputations

Like a camera shot
came a flash of light
Sparkling dimly
throughout the night

Window panes shattered
Reflecting no more
Lifeless and inane
A shadowy rapport

Between all conflict
A love so sure
Conquering madness
Truthful ever more

Confusion reigns
Revulsion in heartache
Streets oozed with pain
A solitary snowflake

Crimson rivers flowing
Welling with glee
Ugliness, revulsion
Sweetest effigy

Nocturnal Sunrise
ALISON STRANGE-GREEN

Shimmering

With shivering dread
came a cool empty stare
Remorse of the days
in which you cared

Forever this passion
was meant to last
Shattered and damaged
broken glass

Now all revealed
in a poisonous zeal
Heartfelt displeasure
A loathing so real

Dancing through snowstorms
A dazzling light
Past a timeless future
It penetrates life

Tearing through souls
to always return
Unwelcomed consciousness
Darkest truth unearthed

Nocturnal Sunrise
ALISON STRANGE-GREEN

Smile

You created the sadness in my smile
The darkness in my eyes
No longer through the misty rain
are images worthwhile

Unlike a stained glass window
I forget to sparkle and shine
Darkness sets and evening falls
Remorse and fear come alive

Revelling in beauty
from the radiance within
Mirrored pool of rustic light
Regrets of pain and sin

Yesterday a painful past
Tomorrow moments to abide
Celebrating every moment
when you made me smile

Nocturnal Sunrise
ALISON STRANGE-GREEN

Sword

An epitaph
of lovers mourned
Shadows weep
Sadness falls

Frozen thoughts
pass though time
A memory
of love worthwhile

Touched by sorrow
Her sharpened sword
Love regained
before each dawn

Heartfelt passions
from deep within
Ebbing ever closer
united in sin

Nocturnal Sunrise
ALISON STRANGE-GREEN

The Abyss

Crystal shadows flow through my thoughts
only to fall true
Many clear memories
Oceans of grey and blue

Your empty eyes now hollow
Debris cast at sea
Shallow eyes are paralysed
with vivid imagery

Darken passages reflect the view
Calling at every door
Turn and meet your conscience
Reflecting memories once more

Within the scarlet moonlit sky
Compassion turned to dread
Rustic hills of daffodils
Creatures left for dead

Wallow in your selfish cries
Men are lost at sea
Creation is your own abyss
A reviled memory

Nocturnal Sunrise
ALISON STRANGE-GREEN

The Cascade

Sounds of the river
echo through time
Many thoughts turn
to the raindrop that cries

Endless and empty
footsteps in the snow
Imprinted forever
Each moment so slow

Each sacred vision
a shadowy grace
Shallow words spoken
My loyalty misplaced

A longing inside
of loathing and dread
Comparisons hurtful
For you I wish death

Taking their toll
each half backward glance
Never understanding
the fact that you're damned

Nocturnal Sunrise
ALISON STRANGE-GREEN

Drawn in paradise
together in pain
Forever a memory
Nothing is gained

Depth of the ocean
Solace of the stars
A heartbeat is broken
Its torn apart

Sacred souls broken
Never repaired
Angels without wings
A world without air

Expressions on faces
Melting sunshine
Never crazed in your laughter
Unhappiness entwined

A measure of misery
which I cannot tell
My empty hallows
My heaven and hell

Following the shadows
Through mystic minds
Lies and the memories
I believe they are all mine

Nocturnal Sunrise
ALISON STRANGE-GREEN

The Howling

Out of the darkness howling came
A roar at every door
Blasting trees of evergreen
Till nature became scorned

Dangerous days of passing moons
cast their ugly spell
Vibrant lights turned ashen
Till the dawn it rose in hell

Desolate lands captured
ravaged by the immortal beast
Demolished cities turned to stone
The lamenting howling ceased

Nocturnal Sunrise
ALISON STRANGE-GREEN

Frosted

Reaching into wonder
A place without pain
Many fools laughed and died
Trembling hearts the same

Clouded pointers of the past
Frosted window panes
Disappear into madness
never to be reclaimed

Nocturnal Sunrise
ALISON STRANGE-GREEN

Harmony

Fractured smiles
The moon it cries
Swollen rivers
run red with lies

Replaced with lives
of sickening sorrow
Reflections of yesterday
Nothingness tomorrow

Slowly drifting apart
So mindful and clear
Cherished times replaced
by indifference and fear

Nocturnal Sunrise
ALISON STRANGE-GREEN

The Bedroom

Each key it slowly turned
Bedrooms of my mind
Conscious act of madness
slowly locked aside

Fallen days of happiness
reside throughout my soul
Effervescent beauty
replaced by an empty hole

Agony is hard to see
unless in my mind you dwell
Crippling conflict presented
Happiness in hell

Suffering between
each moral memory
Seeks solace, solitude and forgiveness
eclipsing all you dreamt of me

Nocturnal Sunrise
ALISON STRANGE-GREEN

Crashed

Awash with tragedy
Photographs forever framed in fate
Pictures of days with sunlight rays
Of sculptures in the sands

Dusty, dreary sandy dews
A tranquil idyllic scene
Comparisons of another world
Perfection within a dream

Lonely are these memories
Do I ponder these alone?

Perhaps you cross the rocky shores
to only think of me
A castle vanished into time
for all eternity

Nocturnal Sunrise
ALISON STRANGE-GREEN

Days

Shallow days of yesterday
flow across my mind
Daily thoughts of love scorned
So cruel and unkind

I never thought I'd love
to ever be so true
Happiness once shared
Love I felt for you

Together waiting patiently
Only time could tell
Memories destroyed everything
Turning heaven into a private hell

A tattered world was left behind
Full of shallowness and shame
All I see are memories
of unhappiness and pain

Some good times that we shared
now tarnished and erased
Covered by a darkened cloud
of jealously and rage

Lifted now has the cloud
If only for a while
Thoughts now turn forward
where you could still be mine

Nocturnal Sunrise
ALISON STRANGE-GREEN

Empty

Tomorrow a day
It falls far between
Forever dirty images
Unhappy and unclean

Never alone
Sadness continues to fall
A picture, an image
Lustful moments, them all

Envy and lust
reflect the calling I saw
Broken and fragmented
Too much revealed in your thoughts

Reflections still linger
within a memorable gaze
Reminiscing in beauty
blissful more innocent days

Nocturnal Sunrise
ALISON STRANGE-GREEN

Frozen

My memory faded
The picture has too
Sun filled lazy days
Laughter with you

Each little moment
We never gave a thought
The moon it shone so brightly
Casting another quick retort

Every smile was taken
Books were left unread
Drunken rugby songs chanted
playing in my head

Each little decision
made in just a flash
Even the big ones made carelessly
though probably quite rash

Photographs are faded
Memories have too
Black and white dreams
of yesterday's time I spent with you

Reflections

Love runs deep throughout the dark
Every twisted creaking door
With every day heartbreak stays
Until sullen smiles reveal no more

Tormented days I dream will pass
Each single broken breath
Turning woefully unto the past
Until nothing sacred is left

Remains of tuneful melodies
Sights and sounds fade fast
Shadows left parallels
A eulogy of the past

Nocturnal Sunrise
ALISON STRANGE-GREEN

41

Tortured

Deepest breath, a silent sigh
makes me think of you
Strength behind my blinding fear
Love so tarnished, forever true

Each painful blissful glance we share
A perfect memory
Your lazy gaze, subtle smile
Intentions seemed so real

Through every day love passes
Collections of our embrace
Pure, sweet and clean
Timeless and desolate

Each gaze cast upon my mind
My love for you reclaimed
A light within that flickers
Devoted eternal flame

To give myself to you
A humble sign of faith
I have trust in you forever
For you I give my life

Twisted

Shed a tear silently
Care just as I do
Heartless days of pain
Misery I spent with you

Tortured children of our past
Each sordid story read
Our misery a twisted pain
of togetherness unshared

Remembering times of happiness
Of how much you cared
A love forever lasting
Just you being there!

Nocturnal Sunrise
ALISON STRANGE-GREEN

Solitude

Bangalore Christian Cemetery

Blaenconin Baptist Church, Llandysillio

Mischievous Gargoyle

Thoughtful

Delusions

Forever secured by inadequacies
My imitation angel
Swaying in the breeze
Never alive nor are you dead
Staring into the abyss
Self-loathing in dread

Devilish images caught up in your soul
Too much for many
You're always alone
Beauty of solitude brings its rewards
Peace and tranquillity
Delusions you sought

Floral tributes at a mocked up grave
Reflect the obstacles
Eclectic choices you made
Such as in life it's a past memory
Our future has faded
Flittered into the breeze

Nocturnal Sunrise
ALISON STRANGE-GREEN

Deity

"Symbolic icons of the past
forever exists in stained glass
Memories within your head
Iconic depictions of the living and dead"

Nocturnal Sunrise
ALISON STRANGE-GREEN

Cherubs

Watching angels as they sleep
A precious selfless act
Lifeless days in meadows
Beyond life's eternal trap

Destiny spun its web
Children watched in awe
Images of demons
reared their heads once more

Understanding empathy
Revelling in woe
Connected between sadness
Angels flew once more

Angelic views of cherubs
drifting through the skies
Church bells cease to toll
Hidden by the lies

Cupid turned with grace
Casting arrows though the sky
Landing ever faithlessly
No hope though all the lies

Nocturnal Sunrise
ALISON STRANGE-GREEN

Euphoria

"Cherubs called the heavens
Celestial skies above
Turning sorrow into euphoria
Pure hatred into love"

Nocturnal Sunrise
ALISON STRANGE-GREEN

Church

Winding golden spires
Reach unto the skies
Shades of blue and gold
Creation of a lie

Beauty within sadness
Happiness in grief
Change its path so swiftly
A secret held beneath

Forever an imposing place
filled with joyful tears of dread
Each tower clambers waywardly
Memories relived

In death a place of solitude
Each life a new resource
Masking ugliness with beauty
In faith forever more

Nocturnal Sunrise
ALISON STRANGE-GREEN

Hope

Eternity is another word
for bitterness and hate
Created slowly in a vacuum
Destruction in its wake

Destroying all I had
Everything in me
Twisted life of hopelessness
One of repulsion and misery

Morality is another word
you never understood
Sacrificing everything
held dear in my thoughts

Nothing could be sacred
Calamity it stayed
Lost to conflict and comparisons
Destroyed in every way

Nocturnal Sunrise
ALISON STRANGE-GREEN

Leaves

Leaves adorned your mottled brow
The saddest sullen days
Visions running forwards
of our yesterdays

Tomorrow never came for you
Fate stopped you whilst you slept
In lovers' arms you faded
Leaving pride and loneliness

Together now alone in death
To love you as I do
Sharing special memories
My mission seems untrue

For now a mournful entity
A merciful goodbye
No longer visions flow here
One final whimpering cry

Nocturnal Sunrise
ALISON STRANGE-GREEN

Salvation

The doors of salvation
Angels spread their wings
Casting charitable hope
amongst tragic earthlings

Fallen from grace
An angelic demise
Tattered and ravaged
Forever lost in time

Angels of darkness
flutter their wings
Reinforced by beauty
Ultimately scarred by true sin

Creeping to the cross
Passing several watery graves
Mournfully caught each impure gaze
Visionary sights of lesser mortals saved

Soulless

I need you with each waking hour
I need you in your sleep
Treasured moments of yesterday
run forever deep

Soulless passions passing through
visions in my mind
An effigy of love and dreams
grasping within a world unkind

Evil demons of the past
cease to shimmer and fade
If love is everlasting
Memories won't stay

Tomorrow is another day
I shall spend so true
Rebuilding special moments
of time in hell with you

Nocturnal Sunrise
ALISON STRANGE-GREEN

The Mist

Angelic views shattered
of what you mean to me
No more thoughtful days of old
Togetherness or serenity

The past it plays the present
In each life we live
No more precious moments
Only intentions to forgive

Meandering through the days
My empty heart it wanes
No longer waves of passion
Or passionate embrace

A life that's lived but compromised
In every single way
Drifting wayward our happiness
The mist slowly ebbs away

Nocturnal Sunrise
ALISON STRANGE-GREEN

Innocence

St Cledwyn's Church, Llanglydwen

Strength

Bedwellty Church, Coed Duon

Bangalore Christian Cemetery

Crucifixion

To haunt you in your nightmares
To hunt you in your dreams
To fear me an obligation
No one will hear you scream

You tortured me when in life
My infliction plain to see
Now in death I crucify you
Creating sorrow and misery

Shallow empty choices made
I shall change their course
Passion turns to hatred
You shall be no more

Nocturnal Sunrise
ALISON STRANGE-GREEN

Depictions

Depictions of creatures
fall through the skies
Emptiness follows
a harrowing cry

Warm and so tender
Wounded they lie
Beauty of death
Your love so worthwhile

Many moons pass
A memory that fades
Together in harmony
Tragedy stays

Bleeding through heartache
Long deadly gaze
So positive and mild
Warm violent haze

Feel this emotion
Weakness so strong
Each moment eternity
Your love does no wrong

Nocturnal Sunrise
ALISON STRANGE-GREEN

Deathly and shallow
thoughts in my mind
Together embrace
Betrayal of sunshine

Sparkling rays
Images of you
Wonder in splendour
Each thought is so true

Nocturnal Sunrise
ALISON STRANGE-GREEN

Grin

I wallow in your misery
Watch your spirits fall
Turn your thoughts to ashes
Break your soul once more

Grind your bones to cinders
Laugh and watch you bleed
Cripple you with fear
Things you've done to me

Torture your morality
It won't be hard to do
Sickening tales of carnality
Spurious images, ugliness of you

Lacerate your being
Pleasure within the pain
Twisted minds between us
Enjoying every game

Open wounded, septic sores
You're only just my prey
A parody of your lust
Existence to be claimed

Maybe when in retrospect
you should have towed the line
Time has passed so ceaselessly
through my razor twisted smile

Nocturnal Sunrise
ALISON STRANGE-GREEN

67

Inferno

Echoes falling through the past
Brief encounter, broken hearts
Never live to reveal the tale
Bodies crumble in life you failed

Darkened halls, oozing death
Accumulating its final breath
Each savage beast it writhes in pain
A fatal twist before its slain

Rotten stench between the walls
Softly carved by a lover scorned
Bodies writhe, flesh it crawls
Infernal beast within us all

Nocturnal Sunrise
ALISON STRANGE-GREEN

Peaceful Revenge

Narrow passages, twisted doors
Sweeping memories, creaking floors
All unveiled to bear a soul
Days of past, each story told

Daily chores fade and die
A love that wells deep inside
Lust and greed stolen all worth
Serving peaceful just desserts

Crevices ignite and burn
Untrusting ways of lovers spurned

ALISON STRANGE-GREEN

Shallow grave

Reaching far unto this lie
Yesterday we fought and cried
This shallow world it reeks of hell
Burning bodies, awful smell

Closing in, each light it glows
Fallen demons cast in stone
Never has it seemed so bright
Darkest hours throughout the night

This is when I think of you
A living death, sickening truth
Tomorrow there will be no pain
No restless nights, each day the same

For now it's time to exact revenge
This life I live I can't pretend
Another hour, another day
Fantasies of your shallow grave

Nocturnal Sunrise
ALISON STRANGE-GREEN

Spectre

Superior motives in your sight
Darkened days turn to night
Cast in stone and far from grace
Each ugly image your disgrace

Never one to follow light
A spectre looms with glistening fright
Eerily hovering in the mist
Ghostly children meandering

Kettle pot now black with age
Steam it rose to catch your gaze
In death you touch the living dead
A memory inside your head

Spirited thoughts glide you past
Rooms reflect a love that's lost
A future shelved with hallowed dreams
Forgotten love, only memories

Nocturnal Sunrise
ALISON STRANGE-GREEN

The Statue

Full of hope
A glistening rage
Flames flicker brightly
Embers raised

Heartless throng
A sleight of hand
Mysterious statues
carved in sand

Howling winds
An effigy without a face
Blood curdling lust
Your disgrace

Converted beliefs
they drip in sin
Untimely death
Revulsion from within

Burning memories
relived with pain
Churlish putrid thoughts
within your gaze

Mindless action
Blissfully scorned
Presenting woefully regrets
of being born!

Nocturnal Sunrise
ALISON STRANGE-GREEN

Ponder

"A broken body in a broken cage
What happens to me when I reach your age?"

Nocturnal Sunrise
ALISON STRANGE-GREEN

Suffering

If life could be the same
Only for one hour
Turn the clock to happiness
A memory to ponder

Filled with rage and fury
Brewing with pain
Revengeful ways of torment
upon a memory ingrained

Haunting would be far too good
to honour you with death
Repose, pain and cruelty
till there's nothing left

Creating purgatory on Earth
Hell within your life
Crippling you with venom
each day and sleepless night

Nocturnal Sunrise
ALISON STRANGE-GREEN

74

Worthless

Inside this hole a mortal shell
Living nightmare an empty hell
Crucifixion that you craved
Breaking bones each harrowing wail

Smugly swirling towards the crowd
Laughing haughtily quivering shrouds
Celebrated in life but not in death
Removing pity, her final breath

Suddenly a sign of life
A cooling ingot, sharpened knife
Immortality plain to see
Revengeful desires of paralysed dreams

Merrily carving the lifeless corpse
Churlish gestures the weeping sores
Carcass placed in a hole
Buried under memories unknown

Nocturnal Sunrise
ALISON STRANGE-GREEN

Gargoyle, Oxford

Haunting

Mournful Angel. Père Lachaise Cemetery

Bangalore Christian Cemetery

Bangalore Christian Cemetery

The Graveyard

Dulcet tones of urban life
Pierce my ears like a double edged knife
My postcards seem so empty
grey and very bleak
Longing for the mountains
Everything seems terribly cheap

I've made my choices for better or worse
Where I reside an everlasting curse
One more fatality in a northern locality
I cannot see anymore

Society has changed to the point of distain
Through its drones, its dulcet tones
Every street in rubbish knee deep
Lost souls just passing by

Packets and grime, a town lost in time
Well strictly this is untrue
It's urban generation controlled by the bus station
After the sun goes down

Sacred churchyard is it danger at large?
This my primates is true
I admit I sound pious, perhaps maybe biased
It's not the life I aspire to

Nocturnal Sunrise
ALISON STRANGE-GREEN

The Count

To never see your face again
To never see you smile
My world would be a darker place
Your existence makes life worthwhile

To see you crying in the rain
A tortured vivid dream
Painful memories of old
There is no in-between

I will love you always
My heart is yours to keep
My love for you is boundless
For my darkest Count I weep

Nocturnal Sunrise
ALISON STRANGE-GREEN

Chamber

Nocturnal passage ways
Darkening rooms
Burial chamber
gathering gloom

Ice chilled surroundings
with more than fear
I feel a presence
Could you be near?

Gently hover closer
Nearer to death
I hear the imposition
of your deepest breath

The chamber so silent
calming and still
Only glistening droplets
Pools of water menacing

For in this house
Nobody sleeps
They only rest
for a while

Nocturnal Sunrise
ALISON STRANGE-GREEN

No sinister apparitions
of those who died
Cackling, wailing, screeching
or piercing cries

Within this vessel
they finally dwell
Land of the living
between heaven and hell

Nocturnal Sunrise
ALISON STRANGE-GREEN

Not shiny or happy!

The day that music sold its soul
I was twenty one years old
We danced all night to every song
Till that dreaded track came on

Revellers dashed
to the floor
Packed with insanity
Where exuberance called

A clubber tried to take his chance
Bravely asking for a dance
To this I quickly replied
R.E.M. "It's not my style"

Glancing sullenly to the floor
Memories of the track before
Little did I know
that was the day that music sold its soul...

Nocturnal Sunrise
ALISON STRANGE-GREEN

Kings and Queens

Mysterious old fashioned ways
Classic golden crowns
Merriment and frivolity
Jesters and their clowns

Kings and queens revered
Suitors and their maids
Battle scars rites of passage
Majestic courtly days

Behind the shimmering golden jewels
often lay deceit
Courageousness and valour
Merged with adultery of the weak

Crowns eventually toppled
To riotous dismay
Castles turned into prisons
Prosperous captured by their slaves

Envy was forsaken
Suddenly twisted into greed
Paupers reigned with vengeance
leaving carnage in their wake

Nocturnal Sunrise
ALISON STRANGE-GREEN

Serfs rules the land
for a single day
Scattering a legacy of intolerance
indignity and hate

Royal courts diminished
Kings' purses went unchecked
Valiant poor pillaged everything
only the religious veil was left

Doctrine another reason
treating man for his sins
Masquerading as perfection
reasoning at will

Nocturnal Sunrise
ALISON STRANGE-GREEN

Discord

Dirty streets
Forgotten dogs
Abandon trolleys
Urban smog

Shallow place
I do dwell
To some its heaven
It may be hell

Streetlights flicker
A candle at best
Bed in a garden
Junkie in his string vest

Discarded children
without any shoes
Underage drinkers
outside shops for their booze

Ugly street brawls
Petty car crime
Excitement, delusion
This town is all mine

The sadness to this
My town has no name
All battered and ravaged
Each town is the same

Nocturnal Sunrise
ALISON STRANGE-GREEN

88

Hope

Serenity

Bleakness

Trusting

Fearful

Yesterday

Each and every sentence
words went unsaid
Undercurrents of yesterday
Longing never shared

Each page a different story
Ready to unfold
Different views of yesterday
Future hearts so cold

Forever incompatible
Always in a lie
Simple words of yesterday
belong to you and I

Living in a shell
of memories gone by
Emptiness in the shadows
Sadness in each smile

Nocturnal Sunrise
ALISON STRANGE-GREEN

Aching

Heartfelt moments wander by
Drifting slowly ever more
Grasping thoughts of days long past
A keeper at each door

Each door unlocks a vision
of broken unkempt ways
Together in a memory
Vivid thoughts they stayed

Leering though each open door
Truth a vibrant sight
My love for you waned softly
Full of dread and fright

Never was the pain so clear
Each single aching limb
Torn apart and ravaged
Death came from the sin

In innocence distress was caused
Destroying each and every plan
Each door forever open
For the beauty that is damned

Nocturnal Sunrise
ALISON STRANGE-GREEN

Choices

Standing in the morning rain
I looked upon your smile
Wishing you were my saviour
If only for a while

Protect me from this world
Horror and its grief
Hold you in my arms once more
Protect me while I sleep

I watched you slowly without ease
Without a single flicker
Intently looking longingly
My reasoning unclear

A lustful gaze soon turned to love
then fear and revile
For you are just a photograph
from a more joyous innocent time

Everything it changes
Like photos in a frame
Sadness lives within my heart
due to the choices that you made

Nocturnal Sunrise
ALISON STRANGE-GREEN

Crossroads

Crossroads of life where choices are made
Memories suffered, a life betrayed
Illuminating reds turning to green
Horrors awoken as if from a dream

Life a colourful changing bouquet
Altering light transmitting a tale
Array of displays arid yet bright
Dependent on virtues the damage was made

Everything altered with one final flare
Tapered and solemn, eclipsed by the fear
Suddenly dwelling a comfort inside
Choices were made at the Crossroads of life

Nocturnal Sunrise
ALISON STRANGE-GREEN

Devolution

Cloaked in despair
Your memory bleak
Ravaged dolefully
Rejections run deep

Purposely painful
Flippant remarks
Yesterday's thoughts
In life we shall part

The past is the future
Your sanity saved
Revert to the longing
of memories craved

Free from the anguish
Inexcusable pain
A life now complete
with each lacklustre day

Pushing laughter aside
Your future revealed
Tumultuous thoughts
all devoted to me

Nocturnal Sunrise
ALISON STRANGE-GREEN

Distrust

Beauty wore a ghostly charm
Silently sweeping by
Reminiscent of lunacy
Clutching revulsion within its lies

Softly spoken dread poured aimlessly
Imitating sobriety, filthy and unclean
Blind to lust an easy prey
Stolen promises of worldly gains

Taking all you could not see
Dreams last forever in sodden memories
In memorial and praised at will
Obligations feared, sweetness in sin

Distrustful and sullen alone in the crowd
No longer inflicted, destructive or proud
Its finally over; your past lives have won
Dreaming of tomorrow, of yesterday's love

ALISON STRANGE-GREEN

Incantations

Incantations of yesterday
dashed quickly through my mind
Tales of woe and innocence
swiftly left behind

Turning sweetness of the light
into unholy effigies
Disgrace and pity followed
destroying everything in me

Nothing was forsaken
All I saw was dread
Reliving your bygone times
Problems left unshared

The past a present, obvious
Living thoughts in me
Yearning for the yesteryears
Erasing each lonely dream

Nocturnal Sunrise
ALISON STRANGE-GREEN

Normality

Tomorrow never returned its smile
It never became true
Only shallow promises
Nothing was ever pure

Destroying each single moment
Everything we shared
Another entity beckoned
It was always there

Longing for a special place
where all that's yours was mine
It could never have been
during this fruitless time

Sharing was an option
The only chance we had
Bringing with it misery
Darkness in my heart

Living in these shadows
became normality
Nothing different happens
Perhaps maybe in my dreams

Nocturnal Sunrise
ALISON STRANGE-GREEN

Passing

Quilted view of innocence
could never be believed
Turning slowly sideways
revealing a world bereaved

Each single moment lost in space
Never to change course
Deathly thoughts aplenty
Brimming without remorse

Only representing pleasure
Selfless comfort in its place
A life of infidelity
in which loyalties are replaced

Nocturnal Sunrise
ALISON STRANGE-GREEN

Sloth

Only shallow beauty
meant that much to you
Trivial impressions
Never any truths

Look beyond the vanity
Conceited worthless flesh
Objects to desire
before each one left

Lusting over memories
Adolescent to the core
Shallowness in beauty
Each memory is yours

Compete not with youthfulness
ignorance or sloth
Life full of indifference
towards memories of old

Nocturnal Sunrise
ALISON STRANGE-GREEN

Sullied

Moments shared seemed sullied
Precious times reviled
Happiness to sorrow
Heartfelt rendered cries

Every sacred time
reminders of that day
No more dear memories
Time led us astray

Decisions cruelly valid
Choices calmly made
A blanket of unfaithfulness
haunts me to the grave

Never was this world for us
Everything seemed clear
Compassion died long ago
leaving a single tear

Special place deep within
still holds a flickering light
Remembrance of purity
Forgotten, lost from sight

Nocturnal Sunrise
ALISON STRANGE-GREEN

Truth

Tainted truths lie dormant
No truth, now only lies
Eyes a mirror image
of the ugliness inside

Mocking with dishonesty
Feverish distain
Calling for insanity
Another mindless game

Many lies are spoken
to cover up the truth
Fanciful and deluded
Nothingness ensues

Openness is not a choice
Never playing its part
Merging lies with insanity
Disclosing a damaged heart

Nocturnal Sunrise
ALISON STRANGE-GREEN

Wilderness

Knowing lies and tragedies
followed though our lives
Emptiness in pleasure
Truth you can't disguise

Amongst all the sorrow
ignorance and pain
Love forever lasting
Casting misery and shame

Slowly memorising
truths within my head
No trust is formed between us
So many times unshared

Each feeling is contrasted
Blockaded by the view
Reaching far into the wilderness
Today's tomorrow's news

Wounded

Implanted far within these walls
A harsh reality
Twisted thoughts of the eve
that you destroyed me

Before the sadness came the joy
Rejoicing freely the world was mine
Heartfelt tenderness turned to dread
Replaced by insults all unsaid

Never to repair the wound
There will always be a scar
Futures bleak for everyone
Disillusions of who you are?

Nocturnal Sunrise
ALISON STRANGE-GREEN

Despair

Cherubs in Pisa

St Cledwyn's Church, Llanglydwen

Weeping Angel, Bangalore

St Cledwyn's Church, Llanglydwen

Babble

This world it seems a brighter place
It often is quite grey
Envy, sadness and the lust
It still won't go away

Tomorrow maybe different
to forgive is to concede
Never facing problems
My heart it often bleeds

Although today is brighter
My heart it still stays black
Each shallow empty thought
I still recall memories intact

Follow every wanting
Try to change the plan
I could not compete with stupidity
Thy doubt I ever can

I never understand you
I am sure I never will
Your motive so unclear
A life so full of sin

Nocturnal Sunrise
ALISON STRANGE-GREEN

Many waters have passed by
Too many beds been shared
Faithfulness was not a choice
Did you ever care?

As for now a better place
when I think of you
No longer can I compare
with those memories of truth

Nocturnal Sunrise
ALISON STRANGE-GREEN

Blinding Light

Deep within the blinding light
Far within its glow
Each day a love that's stronger
Battling the unknown

If only momentarily
Only for a while
Realisation would reflect
I can make you smile

Each deviant thought lifted
Only never to exist
My love for you is blinded
amongst everything you did

Forgiveness is the hardest thing
Though love you as I do
Some days are bleak and brutal
Deep inside the light is true

Nocturnal Sunrise
ALISON STRANGE-GREEN

Cobbled Road

Many years passed with time
My thoughts faded too
Sleepy bays, shallow waters
Time I spent with you

Now regained within my heart
This memory is true
For blistering rays of sunny days
Evenings I spent with you

Each single boat at harbour
swaying at the shore
Tranquil seas of promises
Idyllic thoughts are ours

Setting sun cast upon your face
Your beauty turned to charm
Memories of togetherness
Forever in your arms

Each rocky, winding, cobbled road
Floral bouquets hang high
Adorning shops and boutiques
Soaring to the skies

A memory is cast inside
A bond shared for a while
Left within a memory
Together falling, forever mine

Nocturnal Sunrise
ALISON STRANGE-GREEN

Dreams

Lifeless strangers passing
A world of empty dreams
Smothered by comparisons
Nothing left in me

Barren hearts flail
Suffocated by the night
Loveless lives are lost
Consumed by a bitterness inside

Created by a memory
Revolving deep beneath
Constant opposition
Endless broken sleep

Shall you flee my mind?
Never does it seem
Twist the clock to purity
A world of empty dreams

Nocturnal Sunrise
ALISON STRANGE-GREEN

Honesty

Stay and wipe away the tears
Watch the world fall down
Tumbling buildings crashing
Laying on the ground

For every man a weakness
Strength in all he sees
Sadly memories differ
Yours not including me

Past a daily present
Always there inside
Many thoughts of wonder
Why you made me cry?

Hurtful and destructive
The fickle hand of fate
Slowly destroying everything
lying in its wake

Still I wipe away the tears
The world came crumbling down
Something good in everyone
Honesty can be found

Nocturnal Sunrise
ALISON STRANGE-GREEN

Regression

Years regressed into days
Moments shared a beholding gaze
Hours now forever long
Isolated memories, Celtic songs

Lasting betrayal
between the days
Bedraggled by memories
Tomorrow's disgrace

Weeks follow closely
Morphed into a dream
Recalling all visions
Each appeared so real

Another year over
Full of heartless remains
Surroundings are stagnant
Nothing has changed

As in the dream
Ever so clear
Another sunrise
Thoughts of you here

Nocturnal Sunrise
ALISON STRANGE-GREEN

Solace

To you I looked in wonder
A life I hoped we'd share
Blissful days reminiscing
Whenever you weren't there

Longing for you passionately
Awaiting your return
To have showed emotion
Of this I now have learnt

My heart it missed you every day
Every tolling chime
Regretful pain between us
Solace now is mine

Reflections of the past
Deniable but true
Illusions of happiness
Harmonious times with you

Nocturnal Sunrise
ALISON STRANGE-GREEN

Sparkle

Each single sparkle
The shining light
Broken fragments
in reach yet out of sight

Alone and empty
The dazzling throng
Envy calling us all
to right the wrong

Many thoughts have passed
A shimmering that fades
Resurfaces and changes
A dawn that never stays

Limitless love from tragic souls
Dark callings from every closed door
Excitement in fear encroaches near
Lost souls are fused once more

Embroiled within hell
Destiny's plan is design
Each slight choice of hand
Emotions of body and mind

Nocturnal Sunrise
ALISON STRANGE-GREEN

Destructive

Deep inside my own mind
I have no return
Confusion reigns the masterful one
Many thoughts unlearnt

My mind an empty vessel
Used and lead astray
Broken, abused and hazy
throughout this relevant day

Empty harbours at twilight
So many shadows fall
Moonlit trees, purple leaves
Misery within them all

My mind is torn and twisted
Set up and out of view
Sense exists no longer
Deceptive and untrue

Shadows

Dreaming of a gentle gaze
A holy memory
Softy spoken humble words
A crippling starlit sea

Each inch a pleasure
A lingering embrace
Longing tender memories
Forever consumed by fate

Gazing backwards graciously
Darkness fell within
Woeful moments tarnish
Reviled in carnal sin

Unable to cast shadows
Reflections fell afar
The mirror whispered eerily
of sinful days gone past

Nocturnal Sunrise
ALISON STRANGE-GREEN

Tears

Lonely whispering hollering sounds
cast across my mind
A void was filled with hollow voices
A longing ebbed inside

Empty vessel full of fear
drained of empathy
Destine sounds in vivid dreams
Thoughts of yesterday

Turning slowly, creeping
an entity drew near
Shadows fell across my mind
Reflecting a single lurid tear

Nocturnal Sunrise
ALISON STRANGE-GREEN

Unfinished eternity

Misty shadows danced across your face
where shadowy gloom resides
Eternal depths of a worldly past
On your face it lies

Fairy dust once scattered
Your flawed yet perfect brow
All that lies is solitude
During every waking hour

A distant, winding crystal lake
A joyous memory
Kept forever within a box
Reflections of you and me

This story needs no pages
for it is mine to tell
Each chapter unravels sadness
Reaching far unto this hell

The most darkened light it glows
However so dim
Heartbeat fades, despair
It shows aimless wonderment

Nocturnal Sunrise
ALISON STRANGE-GREEN

Too many images cascade
Through the valleys above the wind
Flittering moments of memories
Forever bleeding

A ray of hope cast aside
Crippled through the pain
Moments recall happiness
Reminiscent of cooling rains

Nocturnal Sunrise
ALISON STRANGE-GREEN

Summerland

Salvation never far away
Each time a glance was spared
Trusting shades of Summerland
Clambered through moments shared

To stay a little longer
If only in a thought
Recollections cleared the mind
Of silences, distraught

Each time I came to muster
a final long goodbye
Summerland united those
Through the darkest bleakest minds

Turning once unto the light
A spectre plain to see
Two souls became connected
for all eternity

Nocturnal Sunrise
ALISON STRANGE-GREEN

Heinous

I used to pray you left me
Now instead for your return
The milk has turned sour
Leaving curdled memories in turn

The burden has been lifted
Converted into shame
Morning casts its radiance
Existence through our blame

The train has left the station
One final journey home
Broken souls amended
Arrival the unknown

Widows reflect idyllic scenes
Leaves of orange and of green
Autumn branches shedding skin
Reveal brittle truths of our sin

Heinous thoughts refuse to fade
I longed for them to die
Another journey over
My sweetest soul goodbye

Nocturnal Sunrise
ALISON STRANGE-GREEN

Effigy

Translucent faces looking back
Features no longer seen
Forgotten dreams remembered
A ghastly effigy

Suddenly a chill of fear
grappled with my mind
Ugliness bestowed itself
upon this tragic time

Twisted and entwined
If only for one day
Turning back memories
where only truth remains

Nocturnal Sunrise
ALISON STRANGE-GREEN

Oblivion

Rumbling echoes of shallow promises
Razor wire thoughts
Demented features of revolting creatures
Live forever with remorse

Abandoned souls scattered jewels
across the moonlit shores
Causing chaos, greed and revulsion
Oblivion exists once more

Nocturnal Sunrise
ALISON STRANGE-GREEN

Misery

Surly smiles with empty hearts
Braced together within the dark
Once transfixed, your fragile bones
Nothing left inside this hole

Damaged pictures
Damning words
Drifting ceaselessly
towards the deepest hurt

Hollow crimson burning souls
Holding misery to reveal the woe
Each loving day, time fades fast
Bitter memories each thought that lasts

Nocturnal Sunrise
ALISON STRANGE-GREEN

131

Heretics

The hoi polloi came from far and wide
To watch the spectacle from every side
Sickening sights within the streets
Barbaric tortures, blood knee deep

The cluster grew into a throng
Baying for blood to right the wrongs
A righteous roar hailed through the square
Inevitably, the condemned appeared

Gasping each final breath
All hope was gone with nothing left
Their chosen crime was still unclear
It was with certainty death was near

Each noose was tightened around their necks
All bodily functions went unchecked
The stools released beneath their feet
Lifeless corpses swayed in the breeze

The only crime committed here
was one of unbridled fear

Nocturnal Sunrise
ALISON STRANGE-GREEN